Free To Be Vee

Written by: Waterfall Adams

Edited By: Judy Newbern

Disclaimer

Like I said in my debut, self-published book, <u>The Eclectic Mind of Vee</u>, **I AM NOT A RACIST!** Also, the poetry in the book contains topics that are not suitable for immature readers. Reader discretion is advised. And by the way, no copyright infringement intended.

Introduction

I hope you all enjoyed my debut poetry book, *The Eclectic Mind of Vee*. Just like I enjoyed writing and my mom, Judy Newbern, enjoyed editing it. Who knows? These poetry books might be put together in a series of its own. Accepting myself took me a long time to do. It comes with not caring what other people think about me. This time around I want to add some pops of color to this book (it might show up on the eBook version). Something that will make this book catching to the eye. I love to write poetry because to me it is like an art of form using words as a media. Anyway, enjoy the read!

Acknowledgements

First of all, I would like to thank God who is the head of my life. I want to thank my mom, Judy Newbern. I would like to thank my therapist, Charlie Brown. Finally, I would like to thank my fans for your love and support.

Free To Be Vee

It's about time

To be myself.

No matter what everyone says.

That doesn't pay my bills.

Free from society's

So called "expectations."

Free from doubt and underestimating

One's own abilities.

We are all made to be unique.

Facade

Fake it til you make it.

PLEASE!

Ignorance is a thing that will not

Stay blissful very long.

The whole "keep your head down" thing

Does not work for me.

You can't really see

What's going on that way?

Always having to keep

"Up from the Joneses."

They're broke too!

"Keeping up appearances"

A fake image will crack eventually.

"A United Front"

What people think about me,

SCREW THEM!

Telling lies is one thing

But living one is quite another.

You Never Know If

That student you called stupid and lazy might have a learning disability.

Your kid's teacher might have a learning disability.

They don't know what they are doing either.

That heavily tattooed, thuggish looking guy

Is CEO and founder of a Fortune 500 company.

Don't you have a corporate job interview with him?

That pregnant, teenaged girl you called a slut was raped.

That big woman you fat shamed got a thyroid problem.

That guy wearing a pink T-Shirt whom you called gay

Just came back from a breast cancer march.

Which he actually survived.

That burn victim was you laughed at

Survived a plane crash.

Before you judge someone,

Take a good look in the mirror

To see if you are perfect.

If yes, then okay

If not then do us all a favor and...

SHUT UP!

If You

If you can't get a job, create one.

If you don't fit in, stand out.

If you don't know what to do, do something.

If you can't find any opportunities, make them.

If you can't find a home, build one.

If you have no money, make money.

It's better than nothing.

Versatile

Eclectic

Resilient

Original

Nutty

Irrelevant

Creative

Ambivert

Vibrant

Eccentric

Exquisite

How I spell My Name???

Witty

Artistic

Talented

Enticing

Refreshing

Free

Alluring

Lovely

Lively

I don't know about The Salty Peppers.

But I do know about the three elements that make up Earth, Wind & Fire.

I never knew about the Quarrymen, But I do know about The Beatles.

I never knew about 2nd Nature, but I do know about The "T", the "L" and the "C."

I didn't know who Samuel Clemens was, but I do know about Mark Twain.

I hadn't heard of Kenneth Brian Edmonds, But I love to listen to Babyface.

I never heard of Stevland Hardaway Morris, but I revel in the Wonder that is Stevie.

I never watched Whoopass Stew as a kid ,But I did like The Powerpuff Girls.

I hadn't heard of Eric Bishop but I do know about Jamie Foxx.

There are so many Veronica Adams' in the world.

But you are going to know about Waterfall Adams!!

In My Lifetime

I never thought I would see the day a black man would be

Leader of the free world.

I never thought I would live in a world that

Is something out of a dystopian novel.

I never thought I would be living

In quarantine all because of the world's most

Deadliest pandemic and global shutdown.

I never thought I would see a black man's death

Police brutality goes viral.

A shortage in coins.

I never thought I would see people quit their jobs

In large amounts.

But Hey!

I never thought I was to see a black man

Become POTUS

I never thought I was to see a black woman

Became VPOTUS.

And! A black woman becoming…

A supreme court judge of the United States of America!

We Have The Dance (Revised Version)

As a people, we have the dance.

Way back in the Motherland, we always had the dance.

Through times of joy, sadness, to heal and rites of passage,

We always have the dance.

Through times of enslavement, we still have the dance.

Even when they tried to take it away, we danced through the shade.

From the jook joints to the Migration, we have the dance.

Even when it was time to pay the rent, we had to dance.

Through Depression and worldwide war, we have the dance.

In the dance studios and sock hops, we have the dance.

On television and through civil unrest, we have the dance.

Live and in color!

We can get smooth and we can get rough.

Live and in color and integrated!

Through the Soul Train days, and the disco nights,

We have the dance.

With BET, MTV, and VH1 we have the dance.

Through social media, we have the dance.

At Broadway, church, the club, community centers, competition,

Hollywood, television, social gatherings, universities,

All over the world! We have the dance.

We even put our spin on it.

Because of this, I shake what my ancestors gave me

And get my Jackson on.

So, to the future and beyond...WE HAVE THE DANCE!

Queen

Throughout history, people thought that she's a goddess on earth.

I have been known for my beauty,

My style,

My grace,

My class.

I have been known for being

The hostess of the nation

But sometimes, a queen would have to become a king,

Even if it means she would have to get off her throne and

FIGHT!

Besides, in a game of chess

She moves where she wants.

$10 and a dream

It all started in the festival of chocolate delights.

I happen to enjoying the festive activities,

When I saw a booth of opportunities.

They are known for their "calling ladies."

And a few men of course.

They offered an opportunity

To sell a variety of items.

It just started with $10 and a dream,

Even though she lost $10.

It was just a stepping stone.

Mindset

Change the mind from a mind that was

Poor

Poverty

Limited

Closed

Stressed

Slave

And shrift to a mind that is:

Rich

Wealth

Abundance

Open

Relaxed

Free!

Flags of Losers Pt.2

Three flags of evil

Three flags of bitterness

Three flags of ignorance

Three flags of racism

Three flags of hatred

Three flags of...LOSERS!

Which is exactly what they are.

Especially since one of the flags

Was supposed to be a symbol of peace.

One that represented a regional heritage…

Of slavery and racism.

And a flag with the name of a defeated

president who couldn't take the hint.

System

We live in a system that is pretty screwed up.

We have an education system that

Does not really teach about everything.

We have food system that does

Not really nourishing you.

We have a foster care system that

Does not really care about the children.

We have justice system that

Does not really bring justice.

The system works...PLEASE!

You know that woman you have known all your life.

In fact she gave it to you in the first place.

The woman who gets on your last nerves sometimes.

The woman worries about you too much,

No matter how old nor tall you are.

She could be long gone,

You still might be scared of her.

Talk and do all the tough shit you want.

She is still more gangsta than you are.

She is known by many names, but they,

Usually start with the letter "M."

Well, she was not always the woman you see today.

She did not always do what her mama say

Partied hardy, and sexy back in her day.

She had so much fun too!

She probably used to get in a catfight or ten.

There was a time in her life where she would…

Steal her brother's sweater for yearbook photo

Defeat him in tennis

Send her husband running fast.

No matter how big and tall he is.

Besides, the "T' must mean tougher than she looks.

I Would Not Be Here

Mid-1980s

Carpool

Colorism

Cold weather

Ski mask

Thriller

7 months

Next door

Chinese food

A woman's sister not giving a man the time of day.

An average height lady getting with a tall man.

An African American woman getting with a West Indian man.

All these things are why I am here.

There has always been music

That reminds you of your youth.

Music that takes you back to the

Good times you had in your life.

A time of innocence.

Music that the older generations always

Had a problem with and complained about.

Even the government had a problem with it.

Always talking about how its not

"Real Music"

"Not what it used to be"

They shouldn't be too hard on them.

Since they paved the way for our "nasty music" anyway.

But hey! It has been heard about

My grandparent's jazz and swing,

My parents disco and funk,

My Stepmama and Cousins' X's grunge and gangsta rap,

And my Y's crunk and dirty south.

They say the way you move is

"Vular"

"Inappropriate"

"Too sexual"

"Too stupid"

They said the same thing about

My Greatest grandparent's lindy and swing,

My parents' Bump and Robot,

My Stepmama and Cousins' X's Breaking and Crip Walk,

And my Y's Harlem Shake and "Drop like it's Hot".

It's been looked at as

"Too short"

"Too provocative"

"Too revealing"

"Too tight"

"Put on a bra!

Maybe even illegal.

Those things were said about

The generation of greatest pants on women,

The Boomer's crop tops and hot pants,

My Stepmama and Cousins' X's sagging and backwards clothes,

And my Y's low-rise jeans and trucker hats.

Hair of Youth

"Get a haircut!"

They say.

"Too inappropriate!"

They say.

"Too distracting!"

They say.

Even be against the laws of the land,

Because they can symbolize rebellion

But hey! That has been said about

My Greatest grandparents' "Process"

My Boomer parents' "Natural"

My Stepmama and Cousins' X's hi-top fades and rattail

And my Y's micro braids and man buns.

Tech of Youth

Older generations always have trouble,

And often need the assistance of younger generations.

Even though they were inventions by

 Those who came before.

They think young ones are addicted to technology.

That it's a waste of time.

They don't really have a full understanding

Probably think it's evil.

But that has always been said, about

My Greatest grandparents' motion pictures and radio

My Boomer parents' television

My Stepmama and Cousin X's beepers and video games

My Y's social media and internet.

Everybody's Business

When it comes to abuse,

It's everyone's business.

It becomes a hospital's business,

When they treat your injuries.

It becomes a dentist business,

When he or she has to pull records to identify you.

It becomes the court's business

To punish your abuser.

It becomes CPS' business

They will place your kids somewhere in foster care.

It become a funeral home's business

Because as they bury you, somewhere.

No Matter What!

No matter what,

Boom or bust.

People are going to

Dance,

Read,

Eat,

Drink,

Travel,

Have fun

Have kids

Get hair done

Get nails done

Wear clothes,

Watch TV,

Watch movies,

Take that and make money off of it.

Angry Black Woman

YES! I'M ANGRY!

YES! I'M MAD!

YES! I'M PISSED OFF!

SOMEBODY CALL THE POLICE!

THIS BLACK WOMEN HAS LOST HER MIND!

But, here is why.

I'm angry because my kids got sold.

I'm mad because I'm on the bottom of the totem pole.

I'm pissed off because the police killed my husband.

Whenever a white woman is angry,

People listen.

But, whenever a black woman gets angry,

It's a stereotype!

The thing is that, the black woman has been through too much,

She has lost her humanity and her sanity!

Nickel and A Pigfoot

Whether it is a big deal or a little deal,

Simple or complicated,

Conflict can really explode.

Somebody can say the wrong thing,

Even a golden apple started a whole war, once.

No matter what can cause "The Final Straw,"

Someone can end up dead.

It can be something as simple

As a nickel and a pigfoot.

GO BACK TO AFRICA!

In that case,

Let's pack a few things shall we?

We could use some snacks.

Potato chips, peanut butter

Don't forget that ice cream scoop!

Let's take all these spices!

Would go great on this fried chicken.

I'm so parched, I need to quench my thirst.

Let's fill the cooler with,

Beer, Wine, Mint Julep

Even some Jack Daniel!

Hey! We need a playlist for this trip!

Let's put in some gospel,

Some blues,

Some jazz,

Some rock 'n roll,

Some R&B,

Some funk,

Some hip-hop,

Whatever music with drums.

Now! Off to Africa we go!

Too bad we damn near took everything.

Oh well!

Too bad!

We Invented Rock And Roll

From the roots of the gospel,

Grew into some blues in the country.

That has some jump and rhythm of course.

Add that jazz!

Don't forget that boogie woogie!

People tend to forget that

A "king's" hit came from a "big mama."

A church lady give "an architect"

The building blocks to build,

A music that can

Go hard

Get heavy.

Be glam,

Be soft,

Be electric.

Played in a garage,

And have folks,

Rockin' and Rollin'

All over the world.

As a people, we have often been

Copied,

Covered,

Sampled,

Imatiated,

Even though often hated,

Stolen,

Overlooked,

Unappreciated,

Underrated,

Underestimated

And do not get much credit.

I know why Aretha carried her purse,

I understand why Nina had a gun.

It's a must at anything to,

Own our own.

He Reaches You Somehow

So, you love to observe art?

The windows of His houses,

Are stained with colors that illuminate His Light.

And tell stories from His Holy Scripture,

So, you like to read books?

 "The Good Book" was printed

By a press from the revolution of Gutenburg.

You like to listen to the radio,

So a preacher does a radio sermon.

You like to watch television?

So you watch the televangelists.

You are always on social media,

So you see clergy do live streams, podcasts and shorts.

No matter what advances

The older generations think is evil,

No matter where you are....

He reaches you somehow.

(Inspired by "Phenomenal Woman" by and a tribute poem by one of my poetic inspirations, the late Maya Angelou. All credit goes to Maya Angelou)

> She was known for not having,
>
> A supermodel's size.
>
> She was a caged bird,
>
> Who was used and abused.
>
> She understood why that bird sung,
>
> In spite of everything,
>
> Still she rose.
>
> She was also known as Miss Calypso
>
> A Phenomenal Woman was she.

Quotes

Before I go, I would like to leave you with some quotes and words of wisdom from yours truly. All credit goes to the unoriginal quotes. No copyright infringement intended.

"You can find God in unexpected places and you can find the devil in unexpected places."

"God gives the author revised and updated versions.

"Even Jesus used a whip and flipped tables."

"Even though patience is a virtue, it is not infinite."

"Routine can become a rut."

"What's secure is not always secure for long."

"Be there because you want to be there."

"A queen works with what she got."

"You are an artist, you just need to find your medium."

"Life is not all wine and roses except if you are a florist and have a vineyard."

"My book is my business."

"Not all doctors and lawyers are rich."

"Money DOES grow on trees."

"Older generations paved the way for younger generations for better and worse."

"If you can't get a job, create one."

"The only one who controls your career is you."

"NO JOB IS SAFE!"

"A paycheck is a piece of paper that gets lost in snail mail."

"Job security is being at the whims of moody bossy and scheming co-workers."

"The only person that controls your career is you."

"Before you judge somebody, take a good look at your own self."

"Don't forget about yourself."

"The key to making egg rolls is…ROLL!"

"The key to an air fryer is…AIR!

"What Mama doesn't know won't hurt her. And what Daddy doesn't know..forget that he doesn't

need to know.

"When in doubt, IMPROVISE!"

"Shut the fuck up and be grateful."

"Tell your story and expand it."

"The perfect body does not exist."

"Figuring yourself out is a lifelong process."

"Do what works for you."

"Too much and too little can kill you."

"Ignorance is a bigger killer than any disease."

"Parents don't always know best."

"Be your own relationship goals."

"If there's a shortage, look for an alternative."

"People can make fortunes from economic disasters and wars."

"If you think your parents are a piece of work, meet their parents."

"We are all mixed. We just don't know it yet."

"Self hate is a dangerous thing."

"Listen to the children."

"What's the point of getting into the rat race when you can't get on the wheel?"

"In life, have flexibility."

"Keep on learning."

"There is such a thing as new math and new science."

"Sometimes in despearte situations, people do stupid things."

"Humble yourself or life will do it for you."

"History is not boring to those who lived it."

"What goes on in your house can go viral."

"Give credit where credit is due or they sue."

"Elders, respect the young."

"Busy people are often the most lazy."-Robert Kiyosaki

"Life is to short to hold on to long-term grudges."-Elon Musk

"Care about what other people think and you will always be their prison"-Lao Tzu

"Perfect is boring, human is beautiful."-Tyra Banks

"Never dull your shine for somebody else."-Tyra Banks

"You are your best thing."-Toni Morrison

"Education is the most powerful weapon which you can use to change the world."-Nelson Mandela

"Everyone is a genius. But if you judge a fish by its ability to climb a tree, it will spend its whole life thing it is stupid."-Peter O'Toole

"Change is never easy, but always possible."-Barack Obama

"If opportunity doesn't knock, build a door."-Milton Berle

"Truth is powerful and it prevails."-Sojourner Truth

"To accomplish great things, we must not only act, but also dream; not only plan, but also believe."

– Anatole France

"Success is liking yourself, liking what you do, and liking how you do it."-Maya Angelou

"Character is power."-Booker T Washington

 "Freedom is never given; it is won.-A. Phillip Randolph

About The Author

Waterfall Adams is a creative professional who took her destiny into her own hands. Her real name is Veronica Elizabeth Adams. She was born in Paducah, Kentucky and was raised in Mobile, Alabama. She has an Associate of Science in General Education degree from Bishop State Community College and a Bachelor of Arts degree in Art History with a Dramatic Arts minor from the University of South Alabama.

About the Editor

Judy Newbern is a retired teacher. She was born and raised in Paducah, Kentucky. Newbern has a Bachelor of Science in Elementary Education with a Language Arts minor from Murray State University. She is also the mother of Waterfall Adams.

Check out my debut book

The Eclectic Mind of Vee

Available on eBook and paperback.

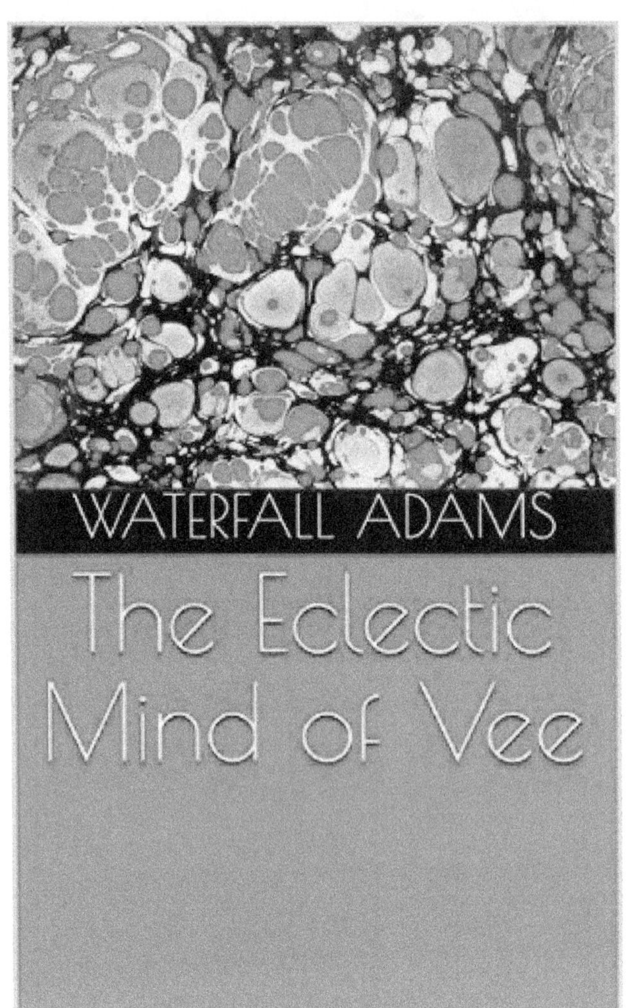

WATERFALL ADAMS
The Eclectic Mind of Vee

Currently available on Amazon and soon to be available on other outlets and maybe available on audiobook.

Check out my blogs as well

Waterfall's World

Waterfall's Online Art Gallery

By the way, follow me on the following social media!
<u>Facebook</u> **and** <u>Facebook page for my blogs</u>
<u>Twitter</u>**:** @vavonni159
 <u>Instagram</u>: @waterfalladams
<u>Tumblr</u>:@vavonni159
<u>Reddit</u>**:**(u/vavonni159)
<u>Tik Tok:</u>(@waterfalladams86)
<u>Pinterest</u>**:** @vavonni159
<u>YouTube</u>: Waterfall Adams

And check Judy Newbern's <u>YouTube page </u>as well.